BLACK PEOPLE IN THE BIBLE

SECOND EDITION

RANDOLPH JACKSON

ORIGINAL ROOTS PRESS
BROOKLYN, NEW YORK

Cover Design
by
DAVID GITTENS

Editor
Amber Burgess-Greene

Second Edition
All rights reserved, including the right of reproduction in whole or in part in any form.

Copyright @ 2013 by Randolph Jackson
Published by Original Roots Press Brooklyn, N Y 11202

Manufactured in the United States of America
ISBN-10: 1489583327
ISBN-13: 9781489583321

Library of Congress Control Number: 2013910879
CreateSpace Independent Publishing Platform
North Charleston, South Carolina

To Sherry Monroe,
with Appreciation
&
Best Wishes.

To Asa Britt and Amir Britt

THE NEXT GENERATION

May the Spirit ever be with you!

Justice Ketanji Jackson

8 Feb 2025

Contents

About the Author ··· vii
INTRODUCTION TO THE SECOND EDITION ················ ix
INTRODUCTION TO THE FIRST EDITION ·················· xi
Chapter 1   Stories From Black People In The Bible ············ 1
Chapter 2   The First Country Named In The Bible Is Ethiopia,
            An African Nation Of Black People ················ 5
Chapter 3   Noah – Father Of Shem, Ham, And Japheth ········ 7
Chapter 4   The Ancient Egyptians Were Black ················· 9
Chapter 5   The Egyptians And The Ethiopians Were Cousins Of
            The Hebrews ······································· 13
Chapter 6   The Prophet Abraham, A Descendant Of Shem And
            The Father Of Three Religions ···················· 23
Chapter 7   HAGAR – Abraham's African Wife ················ 25
Chapter 8   ISHMAEL – The First Arab, A Person Of Color ···· 27
Chapter 9   The Canaanites, The Amorites, And Other Nations Of
            Color In The Bible ································· 29
Chapter 10 Some Other <u>African</u> Peoples In The Bible ············ 35
Chapter 11 Some Other <u>African</u> Places In The Bible ············· 37
Chapter 12 The Hebrews Were A People Of Color ············· 41
Chapter 13 Moses Was A Black African ························ 47
Chapter 14 ZIPPORAH – The Black Wife of Moses ············ 51
Chapter 15 The Ten Commandments Were Received In Africa ···· 53
Chapter 16 Blonde Hair & Leprosy-The Curse Of Whiteness! ······ 55
Chapter 17 The Hebrews And The <u>Canaanites</u> Were Both Peoples Of
            Color And Merged Into One Another ··············· 59
Chapter 18 Black And Beautiful In King Solomon's Harem ······ 71
Chapter 19 Five More Biblical Reasons Why The Early Hebrews
            Were A People Of Color ··························· 75
Chapter 20 The Lost Tribes Of Israel-Found In Africa! ·········· 79

Chapter 21 Two Brown Queens In The New Testament · · · · · · · · · · · · 83
Chapter 22 Black Prophets Of The Early Christian Church · · · · · · · · · 85
Chapter 23 Simon The <u>African</u> Carried The Cross For Jesus Christ · · · · 89
Chapter 24 Jesus Was Black · 91
Selected Bibliography · 95

ABOUT THE AUTHOR

Justice Randolph Jackson

JUSTICE RANDOLPH JACKSON was born in Bedford-Stuyvesant, Brooklyn, New York. He is a graduate of the prestigious Stuyvesant High School (New York City), New York University, and Brooklyn Law School.

After working in the Wall Street firm of (President Richard) Nixon, Mudge, Rose, Guthrie Alexander & Mitchell, he served as a Housing Court Judge, a Civil Court Judge, and a Criminal Court Judge. Justice Jackson was then elected to two consecutive fourteen-year terms as a Justice of the Supreme Court of the State of New York. He retired after thirty years of service on the bench and now practices law in midtown Manhattan.

Justice Jackson is a life member of the NAACP, as well as an author, Bible teacher, empowerment consultant, motivational speaker, and patron of the arts. He has two adult daughters and two grandsons.

Justice Jackson's first book, *How to Get a Fair Trial by Jury*, was published in 1978 and is available at amazon.com and barnesandnoble.com. For speaking engagements, please contact the author at: www.blackpeopleinthebible.com.

INTRODUCTION TO THE SECOND EDITION

Thank you, faithful reader, for braving this second edition of *Black People in the Bible*.

A decade ago, when the first edition went to press, the first black president of the United States had not yet been elected in a landslide. Much additional progress has been made in that decade. However, thousands more are born each and every day. The world's population is soon to reach seven billion souls. With each passing year, a new generation of youth comes of age and must be educated in black history. Those who are unaware of their history are easily persuaded and propagandized that they have none. When I ask myself…. "Why am I here? What is my mission on this earth?" the answers lie within these pages. If you would learn more of the contributions of Black people to Bible and world history, read on. With great humility and fervent prayer for the future, I dedicate this book to my people, my Blessed, Beloved People, all of whom are of African origin.

—*Randolph Jackson 2013 A.D.*

INTRODUCTION TO THE FIRST EDITION

"What is history, but a fable agreed upon?" —Napoleon

THIS BOOK IS WRITTEN to correct the record, which has heretofore been woefully inadequate, concerning the contributions to biblical events by persons of color. In motion pictures, Charlton Heston played the part of Moses and Elizabeth Taylor played the part of Cleopatra, while the actions of people of color went unreported in cinema history.

Yet, the record is clear, to those who read with understanding, that people of color were present and had major roles in the unfolding of biblical events.

The Holy Land stands on the map as a connecting point of three continents: Africa, Asia, and Europe. For many centuries, conquerors, seeking to extend their dominion, have marched across the Holy Land, trampling its people in the process. From Africa came Egyptian pharaohs and Ethiopian generals. From Asia came, among others, the Assyrians, the Babylonians, and the Persians. From Europe came the Greeks (Alexander the Great) and the Romans. Many of the most prominent biblical personalities with whom we are quite familiar were, in fact, people of color. What follows, then, is a clarification in the interest of historical accuracy.

This book also has as its purpose, the raising of the collective consciousness of people of color, who have too long languished under the imposed belief that they have contributed nothing to biblical history.

Generations of people of color have arisen, and fallen away again, unaware that they are the spiritual and physical descendants of princes and princesses; kings and queens; emperors and empresses. Too many youth of today have no knowledge of their glorious past and no notion of their glorious and unlimited future.

Whether or not the Bible *is* historically accurate; whether or not the events described in it actually took place; whether the people named actually lived; these are matters for the professional historians to debate among themselves. We amateur readers of the Bible can take pride in, and enjoy, the ***fact*** that the story of the Bible is filled with people of color.

This book makes no claim of originality. It is an argument and a presentation. The writings upon which it is based are more than 2,000 years old. Through the centuries, these writings have been reviewed and analyzed exhaustively. The yeoman work of modern-day historians and scholars such as Martin Bernal, Charles B. Copher, Cheikh Anta Diop, Cain Hope Felder, John G. Jackson, George G.M. James, John L. Johnson, Richard A. Morrissey, George Wells Parker, Chancellor Williams, Rudolph R. Windsor, and others, deserves acclaim and recognition. If the arguments presented here have been made before, they need to be repeated.

CHAPTER 1

Stories From Black People In The Bible

THE CONVERSION OF THE ETHIOPIAN EUNUCH AND WHY WE NAME OUR DAUGHTERS CANDACE

> Behold, a man of Ethiopia, an eunuch of great authority under Candace queen of the Ethiopians, who had the charge of all her treasure, and had come to Jerusalem for to worship, was returning, and sitting in his chariot read Esaias the prophet.
>
> —Acts 8:27, 28

HE WAS A member of the nobility, the ruling class. We know several things about him. We know he was a black African because he was an Ethiopian. *We* know he was wealthy because he was riding in a chariot while others walked and because he was the Secretary of the Treasury of his country.

We know he was a Hebrew because he was studying the book of Isaiah and because he had come to Jerusalem to worship.

Philip the Evangelist came along and persuaded him to be baptized a Christian.

He then went home and, as an influential member of the ruling class, spread the news of Jesus to Ethiopia. This was the beginning of the Ethiopian Coptic Christian church, one of the oldest Christian churches in the world.

And Black mothers name their daughters "Candace" (or variations thereof) because the word is a title and means "queen" in the Ethiopian language.

THE BLACK MAN WHO SAVED THE LIFE OF THE PROPHET JEREMIAH: EBEDMELECH THE ETHIOPIAN

> Now when Ebedmelech the Ethiopian, one of the eunuchs which was in the king's house, heard that they had put Jeremiah in the dungeon;... Ebedmelech went forth out of the king's house, and spake to the king.
> — Jeremiah 38:7, 8

The Prophet Jeremiah had a major problem. He was in a pit with no water and no food and was near death. Zedekiah, King of Judah, had imprisoned him for making an unwelcome prophecy that had come true. He had spoken truth to power and was paying the price.

To the rescue came Ebedmelech, an Ethiopian, an African and a Black man! Ebedmelech heard of the prophet's plight and went straight to the king and bravely petitioned for the life of Jeremiah. The king was persuaded by the forthright words of this courageous Black man and ordered Jeremiah's release. Ebedmelech then took 30 men with him and pulled up Jeremiah from the pit, thus saving his life.

Jeremiah is one of the Major Prophets, second only to Isaiah. Thanks to the actions of this brave Black man in the Bible, the world now has an additional fourteen biblical chapters in the life of the prophet Jeremiah, as well as the book of Lamentations, also written by Jeremiah.

Ebedmelech the Ethiopian

CHAPTER 2

The First Country Named In The Bible Is Ethiopia, An African Nation Of Black People

And the name of the second river is Gihon: The same is it that compasseth the whole land of <u>Ethiopia</u> (emphasis added).

—Genesis 2:13

THE FIRST COUNTRY named in the Bible is *Ethiopia*. The first book of Moses, called Genesis, tells of the formation of the Garden of Eden. It states that the river that went out of Eden to water the Garden of Eden was known as Gihon. Today we believe this river to be the Nile River. The Bible states that the Gihon River crossed the entire length of the land of Ethiopia.

Ethiopia is clearly a nation of color. The very name "**Ethiopia**" is a derivation of the Greek word aithiops and means "sun-burned faces". The ancient Greeks, in naming the land, also described the people living in it as the dark-skinned people residing in Africa south of the Sahara Desert, bordering on Egypt and the Red Sea.

The earliest human beings were Black. They spread from Africa to Arabia to Persia to India. The ancients knew the entire region bordering the Indian Ocean and the Arabian Sea as Ethiopia, the land of the dark-skinned peoples.

So, we find that the first country named in the Bible is not England, France, Germany, or Belgium, but an African nation of dark-skinned, "sun-burned" people in the land known to the ancients as Ethiopia.

ADAM, THE FIRST MAN, WAS FORMED FROM THE DUST OF THE GROUND AND WAS A PERSON OF COLOR

And the Lord God formed man of the dust of the ground, and breathed into his nostrils the breath of life: and man became a living soul.
—Genesis 2:7

The Bible informs us that the first man was formed from the dust of the ground. As such, the first man had to have been a person of color. For what color is the dust of the ground? Additionally, modern science now concedes that the first woman (Eve) was an African.

CHAPTER 3

NOAH - FATHER OF SHEM, HAM, AND JAPHETH

> And the sons of Noah, that went forth of the ark, were Shem, and Ham, and Japheth: and Ham is the father of Canaan. These are the three sons of Noah: and of them was the whole earth overspread.
>
> —Genesis 9:18, 19

WHEN THE LORD decided to destroy the world by flood, he permitted only Noah, who was a just man, and Noah's family, to survive. Everyone in the world today is descended from Noah through one of his three sons, Shem, Ham and Japheth. Therefore, you who are reading this text are either a Semite, a Hamite, a Japhite, or a combination of these.

Japheth was the youngest son of Noah. The Bible states that he is the ancestor of the people of Asia Minor and Europe. Japheth's son was Magog. Nothing more of the Japhites is heard in the Bible until the time of the end when Japheth's descendants gather to attack Israel.

When Japheth's sons and their families attacked Israel, the Japhites were so soundly defeated and destroyed by Israel that the House of Israel required seven months to bury them. This great battle is discussed in Ezekiel, at chapters 38 and 39.

> Gomer, and all his bands; the house of Togarmah of the north quarters, and all his bands: and many people with thee. To take a spoil, and to take a prey; to turn thine hand upon the desolate places that are now inhabited, and upon the

people that are gathered out of the nations, which have gotten cattle and goods, that dwell in the midst of the land.
- Ezekiel 38:6, 12

HAM, THE FIRST BLACK MAN

And the sons of Ham; Cush, and Mizraim, and Phut, and Canaan.
-Genesis 10:6

The first Black man after the Flood is thought to be Ham. Genesis 10:6 identifies the four sons of Ham as Cush, Mizraim, Phut and Canaan. Each of Ham's four sons went on to found a nation. Ham's oldest son, Cush, founded Ethiopia. Ham's second son, Mizraim, was the first Egyptian. Ham's third son, Phut, founded Libya. Ham's youngest son, Canaan, was the first Palestinian. (McCray, *The Black Presence in the Bible*).

HAM

CHAPTER 4

THE ANCIENT EGYPTIANS WERE BLACK

And smote all the firstborn in Egypt; the chief of their strength in the tabernacles of **Ham** (emphasis added).
— Psalms 78:51

Israel also came into Egypt; and Jacob sojourned in the land of **Ham** (emphasis added).
— Psalms 105:23

They forgot God their savior, which had done great things in Egypt; Wondrous works *in* the land of **Ham**, and terrible things *by* the Red Sea *(emphasis added)*.
—*Psalms* 106:21, 22

EGYPT IS LOCATED in the northeast part of *Africa* and the Sinai Peninsula bordering on the Mediterranean and Red Seas. Ancient Egypt was a nation populated by people of color. Egypt was founded by Mizraim, the second son of Ham and the first Egyptian. Many maps today still refer to Egypt as Mizraim.

And when the inhabitants of the land, the Canaanites, saw the mourning in the floor of Atad, they said, this is a grievous mourning to the Egyptians; wherefore the name of it was called Abelmizraim, which is beyond Jordan.
—Genesis 50:11

The sons of Ham (*Egyptians*) are maligned in the literature of the people they supposedly oppressed (The Hebrew Bible). In the first book of Moses, called *Genesis*, God tells Abraham that the Hebrews would be oppressed in a strange land.

> And he said unto Abram, Know of a surety that thy seed shall be a stranger in a land that is not theirs, and shall serve them; and they shall afflict them four hundred years;
> —Genesis 15:13

The ancient Egyptians belonged to an ***African*** race, which first established in Ethiopia on the middle Nile, and gradually came down toward the sea, following the course of the river. The earliest Egyptians were ***African*** Ethiopians.

The ancient Egyptians always painted their gods black as coal. The Egyptian *Book of the Dead* teaches that the Egyptian gods **Isis** and Osiris are Negroes. The Sphinx is the image of a Pharaoh (king) having the head of a Black man. The profile of the Sphinx *is* Bantu. Cheops, a Black man, built the great pyramid. Menes (or Narmer), first Pharaoh of Egypt, who unified Upper and Lower Egypt, 3,200 years before Christ, was unquestionably black. Pharaoh Tuthmosis III, the Napoleon of ancient times, was the son of a Sudanese (black) woman.

According to Herodotus, the Greek father of history, the Egyptians and the Ethiopians were among the only nations to have practiced circumcision (cutting of the foreskin) from earliest times. The Egyptians transmitted this practice to the Semites (Jews, Arabs, Syrians). It will be seen later that both Abraham and Moses married Black women (Hagar and Zipporah). Circumcision was introduced among the Semites as a result of contact with the Black world.

> "The question concerning the origin of circumcision has only one answer: It comes from Egypt." Dr. Sigmund Freud, Moses and Monotheism, p 29

The social organization of Ancient Egypt was the same as the rest of Black *Africa*:

- The King
- Priests and Warriors
- Skilled Workers
- Peasants

Matriarchy (a form of social organization in which the mother is head of the family, and the children belong to the mother's clan) was found in Egypt and the rest of black Africa. It was never employed among Europeans, Greeks, and Romans.

The Egyptian kings of the 25th dynasty (circa 750 B.C.) were Black Sudanese monarchs. Of the 300 Egyptian Pharaohs, a significant number were of Sudanese origin; some say as many as eighteen. The ancient Egyptians were Hamites by virtue of being descended from Mizraim, the second son of Ham and grandson of Noah. Scholars often use Mizraim's father's name, Ham, when referring to African peoples. Africans are frequently called Hamites. The Bible consistently refers to Egypt as the land of Ham, meaning brown-skinned people descended from Ham.

> And smote all the first born in Egypt: the chief of their strength in the tabernacles of Ham. Israel also came into Egypt; and Jacob sojourned in the land of Ham. They forgot God their saviour, which had done great things in Egypt; Wondrous works in the land of Ham, and terrible things by the Red Sea.
> —Psalms 78:57; 105:23, 106:21, 22

CHAPTER 5

THE EGYPTIANS AND THE ETHIOPIANS WERE COUSINS OF THE HEBREWS

Woe to the land shadowing with wings, which is beyond the rivers of **Ethiopia** *(emphasis* added).

-Isaiah 18:1

And the sword shall come upon Egypt, and great pain shall be in **Ethiopia**, when the slain shall fall in Egypt, and he shall take away her multitude, and her foundations shall be broken down. **Ethiopia**, and Libya, and Lydia, and all the mingled people that Chub, and the men of the land that is in league, shall fall with them by the sword (emphasis added).

-Ezekiel 30:4, 5

In that day shall messengers go forth from me in ships to make the careless *Ethiopians* afraid, and great pain shall come upon them, as in the day of Egypt: for, lo, it cometh (emphasis added).

-Ezekiel 30:9

But he shall have power over the treasures of gold and of silver, and over all the precious things of Egypt; and the Libyans and the *Ethiopians* shall be at his steps (emphasis added).

-Daniel 11:43

> Are ye not as children of the *Ethiopians unto me, O children* of Israel: saith the Lord. Have I brought up Israel out of the land of Egypt? And the Philistines from Caphtor, and the Syrians from Kir? (emphasis added).
>
> -Amos 9:7

THE EGYPTIANS AND the Ethiopians were related to the Hebrews, as they were all descended from Noah. The Egyptians and Ethiopians were descended from Noah through his son Ham and the Hebrews were descended from Noah through his son Shem. Thus, the Egyptians, the Ethiopians, and the Hebrews were first cousins.

Readers of the Old Testament, which is the story of the Hebrew people, are inescapably drawn to the Egyptians and Ethiopians, who were both peoples of color (Dunston, *The Black Man in the Old Testament and Its World*).

Indeed, the last words of the book of Genesis are in a coffin in Africa!*

> So Joseph died, being an hundred and ten years old: and they embalmed him, and he was put in a coffin in Egypt.
> Genesis 50:26
>
> *(Mears, What the Bible is All About)

ETHIOPIA

In the ninth chapter of the Book of Amos, at verse 7, the Lord reassures the people of Israel that He cares for them just as much as He cares for the Ethiopians.

> Are ye not as children of the Ethiopians unto me, O children of Israel? saith the Lord.
>
> -Amos 9:7

> Then the king commanded Ebedmelech the Ethiopian, saying, Take from hence thirty men with thee, and take up Jeremiah the prophet out of the dungeon, before he die.
>
> -Jeremiah 38:10

Ethiopia, an African nation, is featured in many biblical prophecies. It is predicted that at a time when Israel is triumphant, Ethiopia will stretch out her hands to God in adoration.

> Princes shall come out of *Egypt*; *Ethiopia* shall soon stretch out her hands unto God,
>
> -Psalms 68:31

In speaking of the nature and glory of the Church, someone will boast that he was born in Ethiopia.

> I will make mention of Rahab and Babylon to them that know me; behold Philistia, and Tyre, with Ethiopia; this man was born there.
>
> —Psalms 87:4

Isaiah prophesied the destruction of the Ethiopians and the growth of the church .

> Woe to the land shadowing with wings, which is beyond the rivers of Ethiopia.
>
> —Isaiah 18:1

The captivity of the Ethiopians is portrayed by Isaiah.

> So shall the king of Assyria lead away the Egyptians prisoners, and the Ethiopians captives, young and old,

> naked and barefoot, even with their buttocks uncovered, to the shame of Egypt.
>
> — Isaiah 20:4

In comforting the Church with God's promises, Isaiah tells of Ethiopia being given as ransom for the freedom of Israel.

> For l am the Lord thy God, the Holy One of Israel, thy savior. I gave Egypt for thy ransom Ethiopia and Seba for thee.
>
> — Isaiah 43:3

It is prophesied that the Ethiopians shall be subject to Israel.

> Thus saith the LORD, The labour of Egypt, and merchandise of Ethiopia and of the Sabeans, men of stature, shall come over unto thee, and they shall be thine: they shall come after thee; in chains they shall come over, and they shall fall down unto thee, saying. Sorely "God is in thee; and there is none else, there is no God."
>
> —Isaiah 45:14

The prophet Jeremiah foresees the Ethiopian army in battle.

> Come up, ye horses; and rage, *ye* chariots: and let the mighty men come forth; the Ethiopians and Libyans, that handle the shield; and the Lydians, that handle and bend the bow.
>
> —Jeremiah 46:9

Ezekiel twice sees the future destruction of the Ethiopian army [Ezekiel 30:5 and 38:5].

> Ethiopia and Libya, and Lydia, and all the mingled people. and Chub, and the men of the land that is in league, shall fall with them by the sword.
>
> —Ezekiel 30:5

The prophet Nahum mentions a military reverse suffered fifty years earlier by the Ethiopians at Thebes (also known as No). — Nahum 3:8-10

> Ethiopia and Egypt were her strength, and it was infinite;
> Put and Lubim were thy helpers.
>
> — Nahum 3:9

The restoration of Israel is predicted by the prophet Zephaniah, with those who live far beyond the rivers of Ethiopia coming with their offerings. How accurate is this biblical prophecy, made more than 2,500 years ago?

> "From beyond the rivers of Ethiopia my suppliants, even the daughter of my dispersed, shall bring mine offering."
>
> — Zephaniah 3:10

Two thousand years later, the first Black Miss Israel, "the daughter of my dispersed" in the words of the prophet Zephaniah, hails "from beyond the rivers of Ethiopia"! **Yityish Aynaw, Miss Israel 2013**, was born in Ethiopia! Zephaniah was quite a prophet!

In a further vivid illustration of the power and truth of biblical prophecy, *The New York Times* of some two decades ago (March 23, 1991 [page 3, column 2) pictured 20,000 Ethiopian Black Jews in the process of emigrating from Ethiopia back to a restored Israel. That number grew over the ensuing decades to the point that by 2008, the number of Ethiopian Black Jews in Israel numbered nearly 107,000.

EGYPT

It would be impossible to tell the story of the Hebrews without mentioning Egypt, a kingdom in northeast Africa. Egypt is mentioned so many times in the Bible that it is pointless to enumerate them all. Egyptians are mentioned one hundred twenty-three (123) times, from Genesis (Genesis 12:12) to the Apostle Paul's Letter to the Hebrews (Hebrews 11:29).

> Therefore it shall come to pass when the Egyptians shall see them that they shall say, this is his wife: and they will kill me, but they will save thee alive.
> Genesis 12:12

> By the faith they passed through the Red Sea as by dry land: which the Egyptians assaying to do were drowned,
> Hebrews 11:29

The Bible contains at least nineteen different prophecies concerning Egypt. These range from the Hebrew bondage in Egypt (Genesis 15:13), to the plague on Egypt for refusing to come to Jerusalem in worship (Zechariah 14:18, 19).

> There shall be the punishment of Egypt, and the punishment of all nations that come not up to keep the feast of tabernacles.
> Zechariah 14:19

BIBLICAL PROPHECIES CONCERNING EGYPT (AFRICA)

1. And he said unto Abram, know of a surety that thy seed shall be a stranger in a land that is not theirs, and shall serve them; and they shall afflict them four hundred years; — Genesis 15:13
2. And it shall come to pass in that day, that the Lord shall set his hand again the second time to recover the remnant of his people, which shall be left, from Assyria, and from Egypt, and from Pathros, and from Cush, and from Elam, and from Shinar, and from Hamath, and from the islands of the sea. — Isaiah 11:11
3. And the Egyptians will I give over into the hand of a cruel lord; and a fierce king shall rule over them saith the Lord, the Lord of hosts. —Isaiah 19:4.
4. So shall the king of Assyria lead away the Egyptians prisoners, and the Ethiopians captives, young and old, naked and barefoot, even with their buttocks uncovered, to the shame of Egypt. — Isaiah 20:4
5. And it shall come to pass that day, that the Lord shall beat off from the channel of the river unto the stream of Egypt, and ye shall be gathered one by one, O ye children of Israel. – Isaiah 27:12.
6. For the Egyptians shall help in vain, and to no purpose: therefore have I cried concerning this, Their strength is to sit still. —Isaiah 30:7
7. Woe to them that go down to Egypt for help; and stay on horses, and trust in chariots, because they are many; and in horsemen, because they are very strong; but they look not unto the Holy One of Israel, neither seek the Lord!- Isaiah 31:1
8. Egypt, and Judah, and Edom, and the children of Ammon, and Moab, and that are in the utmost corners, that dwell in the wilderness: for all these nations are uncircumcised, and all the house of Israel are uncircumcised in the heart. —Jeremiah 9:26
9. Then took I the cup at the LORD'S hand, and made all the nations to drink, unto whom the LORD had sent me: To wit, Jerusalem, and the cities of Judah, and the kings thereof, and the princes thereof, to

make them a desolation, an astonishment, an hissing, and a curse; as it is this day; Pharaoh king of Egypt, and his servants, and his princes, and all his people. —Jeremiah 25:17-19

10. "And when he cometh, *he* shall smite the land of Egypt, and deliver such as are for death to death; and such as are for captivity to captivity; and such as are for the sword to the sword" — Jeremiah 43:11.
11. "Thus saith the LORD; Behold, 1 will give Pharaoh-hophra king of Egypt into the hand of his enemies, and into the hand of them that seek his life; as I gave Zedekiah king of Judah into the hand of Nebuchadnezzar king of Babylon, his enemy, and that sought his life" — Jeremiah 44:30
12. The daughter of Egypt shall be confounded; she shall be delivered into the hand of the people of the north. The LORD of hosts, the God of Israel, saith; Behold, I will punish the multitude of No, and Pharaoh, and Egypt, with their gods, and their kings; even Pharaoh, and all them that trust in him. —Jeremiah 46:24, 25.
13. Son of man, set thy face against Pharaoh king of Egypt, and prophesy against him and against all Egypt. —Ezekiel 29:2.
14. And the king of the south shall be strong, and one of his princes; and he shall be strong above him, and have dominion; his dominion shall be a great dominion. And shall also carry captives into Egypt their gods, with their princes, and with their precious vessels of silver and of gold; and he shall continue more years than the king of the north, —Daniel 11:5, 8.
15. They shall not dwell in the LORD'S land; but Ephraim shall return to Egypt, and they shall eat unclean things in Assyria. Hosea 9:3.
16. When Israel was a child, then I loved him, and called my son out of Egypt. --Hosea 11:1
    A reference to Jesus contained in the Old Testament! See Matthew: 2:15.
17. Egypt shall be a desolation, and Edom shall be a desolate wilderness, for the violence against the children of Judah, because they have shed innocent blood in their land. —Joel 3:19.

18. I will bring them again also out of the land of Egypt, and gather them out of Assyria; and I will bring them into the land of Gilead and Lebanon and place shall not be found for them. -- Zechariah 10:10.
19. This shall be the punishment of Egypt, and the punishment of all nations that come not up to keep the feast of tabernacles. —Zechariah 14:19

CHAPTER 6

THE PROPHET ABRAHAM, A DESCENDANT OF SHEM AND THE FATHER OF THREE RELIGIONS

> These are the generations of Shem: Shem was an hundred years old, and begat Arphaxad two years after the flood.
> — Genesis 11:10

> And Terah lived seventy years, and begat Abram, Nahor, and Haran.
> —Genesis 11:26

THE OLDEST SON of Noah was Shem. He is thought to be the ancestor of the Semitic peoples. The best-known Semitic peoples today are the Arabs, the Jews and the Syrians. The descendants of Shem went to Arabia and Palestine. They settled the greater part of southwest Asia. Today, the Semites are those who speak Semitic languages.

The ancient Hebrews were Semites. The Arabs and some Ethiopians are modern Semitic-speaking peoples. The Bible tells us how Abraham, whose name was changed by God from Abram to Abraham, was descended from Shem and was, therefore, a Semite (Genesis 11).

From Abraham, a Semite, descended three great religions —Judaism, Christianity and Islam. Abraham was the first Hebrew and the father of

Judaism. Jesus Christ, the founder of Christianity, was descended from Abraham.

> The book of the generation of Jesus Christ, the son of David, the son of Abraham.
> —Matthew 1:1

The Prophet Muhammad, the founder of the Muslim religion, claimed to be descended from Abraham through Ishmael, Abraham's <u>oldest</u> son.

CHAPTER 7

HAGAR
Abraham's African Wife

Now Sarai Abram's wife bare him no children; and she had a handmaid, an Egyptian, whose name was Hagar.
And Sarai said unto Abram, Behold now, the Lord hath restrained me from bearing: I pray thee, go in unto my maid;

it may be that I may obtain children by her. And Abram hearkened to the voice of Sarai.

And Sarai Abram's wife took Hagar her maid the Egyptian, after Abram had dwelt ten years in the land of Canaan, and gave her to her husband Abram to be his *wife* (emphasis added).

— Genesis 16:1-3

CHAPTER SIXTEEN OF the book of Genesis informs us that Abraham took a second wife when his first wife, Sarah, could have no children. His second wife was an Egyptian woman named Hagar. She was the maid of Sarai.

As we have previously learned, the Egyptians were an African people of color, descended from Ham, the first Black man. The Egyptians were called Hamites.

Hagar, Abraham's second wife, was an Egyptian, an African, and a Black woman!

CHAPTER 8

ISHMAEL-THE FIRST ARAB, A PERSON OF COLOR

And Hagar bare Abram a son; and Abram called his son's name, which Hagar bare, **Ishmael** (emphasis added).

—Genesis 16:15

And as for Ishmael, I have heard thee: Behold, I have blessed him, and will make him fruitful, and will multiply him exceedingly; twelve princes shall he beget, and I will make him a great nation (emphasis added).

—Genesis 17:20

ABRAHAM, THE FIRST Hebrew, from the Asian land of Mesopotamia, took as his second wife, an African Negro girl, named Hagar (Genesis 16:1). They had a brown son named Ishmael, the first Arab. Ishmael was the first Arab and was a person of color. He was born to Abraham by Abraham's second wife, Hagar, an Egyptian African woman. He was born when Abraham was eighty-six years of *age*. He was the elder son of Abraham. The Lord promised Abraham that Ishmael had been blessed and would be fruitful and would multiply exceedingly (Genesis 17:20). He would beget twelve princes and the Lord promised to make him a great nation. Ishmael married an African.

And he dwelt in the wilderness of Paran: and his mother took him a wife out of the land of Egypt (emphasis added).

—Genesis 21:21

Thus, Ishmael was the son of a black *African* Egyptian woman and was the husband of a black *African* Egyptian woman.

Their twelve sons established a tribe known as the Ishmaelites.

> And these are the names of the sons of Ishmael, by their names, according to their generations: the firstborn of Ishmael, Nebajoth; and Kedar, and Adbeel, and Mibsam. And Mishma, and Dumah, and Massa, Hadar and Tema, Jetur, Naphish, and Kedemah: These are the sons of Ishmael, and these are their names, by their towns, and by their castles; twelve princes according to their nations.
>
> Genesis 25: 13-16

The prophet Muhammad, the founder of Islam, claimed to be descended From Ishmael. The Ishmaelites, or as we call them, Arabs, who live chiefly in Arabia and in North Africa are often referred to as Semites, because their language, Arabic, belongs to the Semitic group of languages.

CHAPTER 9

THE CANAANITES, THE AMORITES, AND OTHER NATIONS OF COLOR IN THE BIBLE

And the sons of Ham: Cush, and Mizraim, and Phut, and Canaan. And Canaan begat Sidon, his first born, and Heth, and the Jebusite, and the Amorite, and the Girgasite, and the Hivite, and the Arkite, and the Sinite, And the Arvadite, and the Zemarite, and the Hamathite: and afterward were the families of the Canaanites spread abroad. And the border of the Canaanites was from Sidon, as thou comest to Gerar, unto Gaza; as thou goest, unto Sodom, and Gomorrah, and Admah, and Zeboim, even unto Lasha. These are the sons of Ham, after their families, after their tongues, in their countries, and in their nations (emphasis added).

—Genesis 10:6, 15-20

There are other nations of color named in the Bible, including, but not limited to, the Canaanites and the Amorites. Canaan was the youngest son of Ham, the first Black man.

The Canaanites lived in the region later known as Palestine. They belonged to the same race of people as the Arabs, the Assyrians, and the Hebrews. —Genesis 10:19

The Amorites were descendants of Canaan. They, too, were children of Ham—the first Black man and they were people of color.

> And Canaan begat Sidon his firstborn, and Heth, and the Jebusite and the Amorite, and the Girgasite.
> —Genesis 10:15, 16

THE EDOMITES ARE descended from Esau (the son of Isaac) and his several wives (Genesis 36:1). Esau married Canaanite (brown) women and Arab (brown) women. His Arab wives were his first cousins, Bashemath and Mahalath, daughters of his uncle, Ishmael, Abraham's son.

> Then went Esau unto Ishmael, and took unto the wives which he had Mahalath the daughter of Ishmael Abraham's son, the sister of Nebajoth, to be his wife.
> —Genesis 28:9

> Esau took his wives of the daughters of Canaan; Adah the daughter of Elon the Hittite, and Aholibamah the daughter of Anah the daughter of Zibeon the Hivite; and Bashemath Ishmael's daughter, sister of Nehajoth.
> —Genesis 36:2, 3

As we have seen, their mother, Ishmael's wife, was an African (Genesis 21:21) and so was their grandmother, Hagar (Genesis 16:1, 15).

Esau's Canaanite wives included *Judith*, daughter of Beeri the Hittite.

> And Esau was forty years old when he took to wife Judith the daughter of Berri the Hittite, and Bashemath the daughter of Elon the Hittite.
>
> —Genesis 26:34

Adah is the daughter of Elon the Hittite, and Aholibamah is the daughter of Anah, who is the daughter of Zibeon the Hivite (Genesis 36:2).

The Hittites, The Canaanites, The Amorites, and other nations of color in the Bible are descended from Heth, a son of Canaan.

> And Canaan begat Sidon his firstborn, and Heth.
>
> —Genesis 10:15

The Hivites are also a nation descended from Canaan (Genesis 10:17).

THE JEBUSITES
(THE ORIGINAL INHABITANTS OF JERUSALEM)

> And David and all Israel went to Jerusalem, which is Jebus; where the Jebusites were, the inhabitants of the land.
>
> — I Chronicles 11:4

Jebus was the original name of Jerusalem.

> But the man would not tarry that night, but he rose up and departed, and came over against Jebus, which is Jerusalem; and there were with him two asses saddled, his concubine also was with him.
>
> —Judges 19:10

The original inhabitants of the *city, Jebus* (Salem), were known as the *Jebusites*, a nation of color descended from Canaan (Genesis 10:16). The Jebusites were both children of Ham and Canaanites (Genesis 10:15, 16).

Please note well the derivation of the place name Jerusalem: Jebus (Salem) = Jerusalem.

An important place in biblical history is occupied by Melchizedek, King and Priest of <u>Salem</u> (Jerusalem). Before Abraham was Abraham, when he was still known as Abram, Melchizedek blessed him and, as tokens of friendship and hospitality, supplied Abraham and his men with refreshment and sustenance.

> For this <u>Melchisedec</u>, king of Salem, priest of the most high God, who met Abraham returning from the slaughter of the kings, and blessed him; Now consider how great this man was, unto whom even the patriarch Abraham gave the tenth of the spoils (emphasis added).
> —Hebrews 7:1, 4

Later Melchizedek is compared to Jesus Christ as a priest forever, of the highest rank.

> Whither the forerunner is for us entered, even Jesus, made an high priest for ever after the Order of Melchizedek.
> — Hebrews 6:20

This Melchizedek was the Canaanite King of Jerusalem before it was Jerusalem, when it was Urusalim (Salem for short). He was a Canaanite, a Jebusite, and a Black man.

> And Melchizedek king of Salem brought forth bread and wine: and he was the priest of the most high God. And he blessed him, and said, Blessed be Abram of the most high God, possessor of heaven and earth: And blessed be the

> most high God, which hath delivered thine enemies into thy hand. and he gave him tithes of all.
> —Genesis 14:18-20

The Temple of David was later built on the site of the threshing floor of Ornan the Jebusite, a Black man.

> Then the angel of the LORD commanded Gad to say to David, that David should go up, and set up an altar unto the LORD in the threshing floor of Ornan the Jebusite.
> — I Chronicles 21:18

CHAPTER 10

SOME OTHER AFRICAN PEOPLES IN THE BIBLE

Come up, ye horses; and rage, *ye* chariots, and let the mighty men come forth; the Ethiopians and the *Libyans*, that handle the shield, and the *Lydians*, that handle and bend the bow (emphasis added). With twelve hundred chariots, and [three score thousand horsemen: and the people were without number that came with him out *of* Egypt; the *Lubims, the Sukkims,* and the *Ethiopians* (emphasis added).

—2 Chronicles 12:3

HERE ARE SOME additional African peoples our Bible cites:

Anamim	A people of northern Egypt	Genesis 10:13
Chub	Allies of Egypt, an African nation.	Ezekiel 30:5
Cyrenian	A native of Cyrene, an African city.	Mark 15:21, Luke 23:26, Acts 6:9
Libyans	Inhabitants of Libya, an African nation.	Jeremiah 46:9, Daniel 11:43 and 16;8
Lubims	An African race.	2 Chronicles 12:3
Lydians	A people of North Africa	Jeremiah 46:9 and Ezekiel 30:5
Naphtuhim	Inhabitants of central Egypt	Genesis 1 0:13
Sukkims	An Egyptian tribe	2 Chronicles 12:3
Zuzims	A tribe in the land of Ham	Genesis 14:5

CHAPTER 11

SOME OTHER AFRICAN PLACES IN THE BIBLE

> And it shall come in pass in that day, that the Lord shall set his hand again the second time to recover the remnant of his people, which shall he left, from Assyria, and from Egypt, and from Pathros, and from Cush, and from Elam, and from Shinar, and from Hamath, and from the islands of the sea.
>
> Isaiah 11:1

OUR HOLY BIBLE is crowded with references to place names located in Africa. The reader is encouraged to maintain close at hand a Bible Atlas (book of maps) and a Concordance of the Bible (alphabetical listing of all words contained in the Bible). Set forth below is a partial listing of African places mentioned in the Holy Bible.

Alexandria	A City in Egypt	Acts 18:24, 27:6, and 28:11
Cush	The land of the descendants of Cush, eldest son of Ham	Isaiah 11:11
Cyrene	A City in the *African* nation of Libya	Acts 13:1
Dizahab	A place in the Sinai wilderness (Egypt)	Deuteronomy 1:1
Egypt	A kingdom in northeast *Africa*. Mentioned in the holy bible more than 200 times.	
Ethiopia	The land south of Egypt. Mentioned in the holy bible forty times.	
Gihon	A river in the Garden of Eden (believed to be the Nile)	Genesis 2:13
Goshen	A district of Egypt. Mentioned twelve times.	Genesis 45:10, Exodus 9:26
Hanes	A place in Egypt	Isaiah 30:4
Horeb	A mountain range in Sinai (Egypt). Mentioned seventeen times	Exodus 3:1
Jeshimon	A place in the Sinai (Egypt)	Malachi 4:4; Numbers 21:20 and 23:28
Libya	A land in northern *Africa*	Ezekiel 30:5 and 38:5; Acts 2:10
Memphis	A city in the *African* nation of Egypt	Hosea 9:6
Migdol	A place in northern Egypt	Jeremiah 44:1 and 46:14
Noph	A city in Egypt	Isaiah 19:13; Jeremiah 44:1; 46:14 and 46:19 Ezekiel 30:13 and 30:16

On	An ancient city in northern Egypt on the Nile Delta, also known as Heliopolis	Genesis 41:45
Pathros	A name for upper Egypt (now known as Sudan), an *African* nation	Isaiah 11:11
Phut	The land of the descendants of Phut, the third son of Ham and the ancestor of the Libyans	Ezekiel 27: 1 0
Sinai	An area in Egypt (*Africa*) at the north end of the Red Sea. Mentioned 39 times from	Exodus 16:1 to Galatians 4:25
Syene	An Egyptian city	Ezekiel 29:10 and 30:6
Tahpanhes	A city in Egypt	Jeremiah 2:16, 43:7-9, 44:1, and 46:14
Zoan	An Egyptian city	Numbers 13:22; Psalms 78:12 and 78:43; Isaiah 19:11, 13, 30:4, and Ezekiel 30:14

CHAPTER 12

THE HEBREWS WERE A PEOPLE OF COLOR

Now the Lord had said unto Abram, Get thee out of thy country, and from thy kindred, and from thy father's house, unto a land that I will shew thee.

—Genesis 12:1

And Israel dwelt in the land of Egypt, in the country of Goshen; and they had possessions therein, and grew, and multiplied exceedingly.

—Genesis 47:27

> And thou shall speak and say before the Lord thy God, A Syrian ready to perish was my father, and he went down into Egypt, and sojourned there with a few, and became there a nation, great, mighty, and populous.
> —Deuteronomy 26:5

> Now the sojourning of the children of Israel, who dwelt in Egypt, was 430 years.
> —Exodus 12:40

The Hebrews were a wandering Asiatic tribe, who prospered by their entrance into *Africa* (Genesis 47:27). (See Boyd, African Origin of Christianity.)

The Hebrews went into Africa as a <u>family</u> - the extended family of Jacob, third Hebrew patriarch. They emerged from Africa 430 years later as a <u>nation</u> of twelve tribes.

They brought with them African customs and traditions, such as male circumcision and matriarchy, which they had acquired during their centuries-long sojourn in Africa.

> "The question concerning the origin of circumcision has only one answer: It comes from Egypt." Freud, p 29.

Abraham, the first Hebrew, was from Mesopotamia. - Acts 7:2, Genesis 24:10

> "And he said, Men, brethren, and fathers, hearken; The God of glory appeared unto our father Abraham, when he was in Mesopotamia before he dwelt in Charran."
> —Acts 7:2

WHERE IS MESOPOTAMIA? it is an ancient country in Asia between the Tigris and the Euphrates Rivers (Deuteronomy 23:4; 1

Chronicles 19:6). The modern nation of Iraq includes much of this region (Judges 3:8, 10).

The Bible prophesizes that Abraham's descendants would be strangers in a land that was not theirs, that they would be servants, that they would be afflicted for four hundred years (Genesis 15:13, 14).

As we shall see, that is exactly what happened. In fact, the Hebrews lived in *Africa* for 430 years. While in Africa the Hebrews grew from a mere seventy persons to over 600,000 people. When they left *Africa*, they left with great wealth.

Deuteronomy tells the story in one sentence (Deuteronomy 26:5). The Hebrews went down into Egypt "with a few, and became there a nation, great, mighty and populous" while living in *Africa* (Exodus 10:26; Psalms 105:37, 38).

It started with a famine. Genesis tells how many peoples came into Egypt in search of food (Genesis 41:55-57).

> And all countries came into Egypt for to buy corn; because that the famine was so sore in all lands.
> —Genesis 41:57

The forty-second chapter of Genesis continues with the story of how Jacob, the grandson of Abraham, sent his sons into *Africa* to buy corn. While in *Africa*, they discovered their long-lost brother, Joseph, the governor of the land, and the person in charge of the distribution of food. They did not recognize him because he looked just like the other Africans. This is biblical proof that the ancient Hebrews were a people of color!

By the forty-sixth chapter of Genesis, we see that Joseph has invited his father, Jacob, his brothers, and all of their wives and children to join him in Egypt (*Africa*). The total number of Hebrews who went into Africa to live was seventy (Genesis 46:27; Exodus 1:5).

> And the sons of Joseph, which were born him in Egypt, were ***two souls: all*** the souls of the house of Jacob, which came into Egypt, were threescore and ten.
> —Genesis 46:27

Later, the Egyptians made servants of the Hebrews and forced them into bondage (Exodus 1:14, 20-22). This was in accordance with the biblical prophecy made to Abraham many years earlier.

The migration of the Hebrews into Africa (Egypt) was of immense importance, both in the strengthening of the Israelite national consciousness, and through their contact with an already advanced *African* civilization. (See Darkwah, *The Africans Who Wrote The Bible*.)

How long did the Hebrews remain in Africa? The Bible states that they were there for 430 years.

> Now the sojourning of the children of Israel who dwelt in Egypt, was four hundred and thirty years.
> —Exodus 12:40

During that time, there was considerable intermarriage with the Black African Egyptians. Joseph, the son of Jacob, a direct descendant of Abraham, married an African woman, Asenath, daughter of the *African* priest, Potipherah.

> And Pharaoh called Joseph's name Zaphnathpaaneah; and he gave him to wife Asenath the daughter of Potipherah priest of On. And Joseph went out over all the land of Egypt.
> —Genesis 41:45

One of the twelve tribes of Israel, the tribe of Manasseh, descends from their first-born son, Manasseh (Joshua 14:4; 17:10).

> For the children of Joseph were two tribes, Manasseh and Ephraim: therefore they gave no part unto the Levites in the land, save cities to dwell in, with their suburbs for their cattle and for their substance.
> —Joshua 14:4

Another of the twelve tribes of Israel, the tribe of Ephraim, descends from Ephraim, the brother of Manasseh (Genesis 41:52). (It was predicted of Ephraim that his seed would become a multitude of nations. Genesis 48:19) Both Ephraim and Manasseh, founders of two of the twelve tribes of Israel, had an African mother, Asenath.

> And unto Joseph were born two sons before the years of famine came, which Asenath the daughter of Potipherah priest of On bare unto him.
> —Genesis 41:50

At the time that Abraham's wandering descendants—the Hebrews in *Africa — started* on their trip out of Africa, 430 years after they entered, they had increased from seventy Asiatic refugees to 600,000 men of mixed blood (in the words of the Bible, "a mixed multitude) (See Copher, *Blacks and Jews in Historical Interaction: The Biblical African Experience* and Jacobs, *The Hebrew Heritage of Black Africa.*)

> And the children of Israel journeyed from Rameses to Succoth, about six hundred thousand on foot that were men, beside children. And a mixed multitude went up **also** with them; and flocks, and herds, even very much cattle.
> —Exodus 12:37,38

The former wandering Asiatic tribe was now a wandering *Afro*-Asiatic tribe!

CHAPTER 13

MOSES WAS A BLACK AFRICAN

And the Lord said furthermore unto him, Put now thine hand into thy bosom. And he put his hand into his bosom; and when he took it out, behold, his hand was leprous as snow (emphasis added). And He said, Put thine hand into thy bosom again. And he put his hand into his bosom again; and plucked it out of his bosom, and, behold, it was turned again as his other flesh.

—Exodus 4:6, 7

The man Moses, the liberator and lawgiver of the Jewish people, was not a Jew, but an Egyptian
    Dr. Sigmund Freud, Moses and Monotheism, p16.

THE GREATEST HEBREW of all was Moses, the lawgiver. Moses was the Hebrews' fearless spokesman and champion guide. He was the author, under God, of all their ritual and moral legislation.

It was Moses who received the Ten Commandments from the Lord and delivered them to his people.

It was Moses who led the Hebrews out of Egyptian bondage.

It was Moses who parted the waters and crossed the Red Sea. Moses, an African Hebrew, took a horde of bondsmen and molded them in his own lifetime into a compact and vigorous nationality (Deuteronomy 26:5). Moses was born in *Africa. The Hebrews had been in Africa, intermarrying with Africans, for 350 years when Moses was born.*

"And Pharaoh called Joseph's name Zaphnathpaaneah; and he gave him to wife Asenath the daughter of Potipherah priest of On." Genesis 41: 45

> "And the women conceived, and bare a son: and when she saw him that he was a goodly child, she hid him three months. And when she could no longer hide him, she took for him an ark of bulrushes, and daubed it with slime and with pitch, and put the child therein; and she laid it in the flags by the river's brink. And his sister stood afar off, to wit what would be done to him."
>
> — Exodus 2:2-4

Moses was raised as an *African* prince (Exodus 2:19). He looked like an *African* (Exodus 2:19). His foster mother was an *African* princess, who raised him as her own son (Exodus 2:10).

Moses is an African name, given him by his African godmother.

> "And she called his name Moses: and she said, Because I drew him out of the water."   Exodus 2:10
>
> He learned the wisdom of the *Africans*.

> And Moses was learned in all the wisdom of the Egyptians,
> and was mighty in words and in deeds.
> —Acts 7:22

If Moses was learned in all the wisdom of the Egyptians, perhaps it was because he WAS an Egyptian! The great psychiatrist Dr. Sigmund Freud, one of the greatest scientific minds of the 20th century, devoted an entire book to proving that Moses was an African (Moses and Monotheism, Vintage Books, New York, New York, 1939).

> If Moses gave the Jews not only a new religion, but also the law of circumcision, he was no Jew, but an Egyptian. (Freud, p31)

According to the Book of Exodus, the Lord selected Moses to lead the Hebrews out of _Africa_. When Moses protested that the people would not believe him, the Lord had Moses place his hand in his bosom. When Moses withdrew his hand, it had turned white (Exodus 4:6). When he repeated the act, his hand had turned back to its original color. Moses was Black!

Moses

CHAPTER 14

ZIPPORAH
The Black Wife of Moses

> And Moses was content to dwell with the man and he gave Moses Zipporah his daughter.
>
> —Exodus 2:21

MOSES married A Black woman. The Scriptures tell us that Moses' sister, Miriam, and his brother, Aaron, spoke against Moses because he had married an Ethiopian woman —a woman from the land of "sun-burnt faces."

> And Miriam and Aaron spoke against Moses because of the <u>Ethiopian</u> woman whom he had married: for he had married an <u>Ethiopian</u> woman (emphasis added).
>
> - Numbers 12:1

It is clear that the wife of Moses, the greatest Hebrew, was a black woman. The name of Moses' wife is Zipporah [Exodus 2:21, 4:25, 18:2].

CHAPTER 15

THE TEN COMMANDMENTS WERE RECEIVED IN AFRICA

And the Lord come down upon Mount Sinai, on the top of the mount; and the Lord called Moses up to the top of the mount: and Moses went up.

—Exodus 19:20

AT THE LORD'S direction, Moses, the African Hebrew, led the House of Israel out of Egyptian bondage. After traveling for about three months, they arrived in the vicinity of Mount Sinai and prepared to rest. While the Hebrews rested, the Lord descended to the top of Mount Sinai and summoned Moses to join Him. There, the Lord gave Moses ten laws by which the Hebrews were to govern themselves. These ten laws come to be known as the Ten Commandments (Exodus 20:1-17).

> I am the Lord thy God, which have brought thee out of the land of Egypt, out of the house of bondage. Thou shalt have no other gods before me.
> —Exodus 20:2, 3

Moses was with the Lord at the top of Mount Sinai for forty days and forty nights. When Moses came down from the mountain, he delivered to the Hebrews two tablets of stone on which were written the Ten Commandments (Exodus 24:15-18 and 31:18).

> And Moses went into the midst of the cloud, and gat him up into the mount: and Moses was in the mount Forty days and forty nights.
> —Exodus 24:18

> And he gave unto Moses, when he had made an end of communing, with him upon Mount Sinai two tables of testimony, tables of stone, written with the finger of God.
> —Exodus 31:18

Mount Sinai, which is also sometimes known *as* Mount Horeb, is located on the Sinai Peninsula. The Sinai Peninsula is in the northeast portion of Egypt (today called the United Arab Republic) at the north end of the Red Sea, between the Gulf of Suez and the Gulf of Aqaba. Since the Sinai Peninsula is in Egypt and Egypt is in *Africa*, it follows that the Ten Commandments were given to Moses *in Africa*!

CHAPTER 16

BLONDE HAIR & LEPROSY-THE CURSE OF WHITENESS!

> The leprosy therefore of Naaman shall cleave unto thee, and unto thy seed for ever. And he went out from his presence a leper as <u>white as snow</u> (emphasis added).
>
> —2 Kings 5:27

EVE, THE FIRST WOMAN, was an African. All humanity is derived from her and everyone on the planet is, therefore, an African (Diop, *The African Origin of Civilization*; Jackson, *Ethiopia and the Origin of Civilization*). How, then, did so many of us become other than African? The Holy Bible supplies us with answers in the five books of Moses, the Hebrew Torah.

In chapter two of Exodus, we see that Moses, the greatest Hebrew of all, was born in Africa, raised in Africa as the grandson of the African king, <u>known as Pharaoh,</u> and given an African name (Moses) by his African princess foster mother.

> And she called his name Moses: and she said, because I drew him out of the water.
>
> —Exodus 2:10

For an illustration of what an Egyptian looked like in those days, consult the Sphinx. The Sphinx is a gigantic statue with the head of an African king and the body of a lion (Williams, *The Destruction of Black Civilization*). In the fourth chapter of Exodus, the Lord turns Moses' hand white to prove a point and then restores it to its original color.

In the 12th chapter of the book of Numbers, Miriam, Moses' sister, is punished for criticizing Moses for his marriage to an Ethiopian woman. Her punishment was to be turned white for seven days, before being restored to her former color (Windsor, From *Babylon to Timbuktu*).

> And the cloud departed from the tabernacle; and, behold. Miriam became leprous, white as snow, and Aaron looked upon Miriam, and, behold, she was leprous (emphasis added).
> —Numbers 12:10

When the Lord was annoyed or angry with the Afro-Asiatic Hebrews, he punished them *by* turning them white, that is, by afflicting them with the disease of leprosy. Leprosy turns the skin white. When Miriam and Aaron, Moses' sister and brother, became jealous because the Lord had selected Moses to be a prophet, the Lord became angry with them. The Lord turned Miriam's skin white as snow. Obviously, Miriam could not have been white *before* becoming the recipient of the Lord's anger.

In 2 Kings 5:20-27, we are shown another example of the use of the affliction of leprosy as an expression of anger. The story is about the prophet Elisha's servant, Gehazi. The prophet Elisha had cured a wealthy man named Naaman of leprosy and refused Naaman's offer of payment. However, as Naaman was leaving, Elisha's servant, Gehazi, ran after Naaman and accepted gifts from Naaman in Elisha's name. Gehazi then hid from Elisha what he had received from Naaman.

But Elisha, a mighty prophet of the Lord, was aware of what had happened. Elisha punished Gehazi by turning him white. Gehazi and all his descendants were to be white forever (2 Kings 5:27).

> The Leprosy therefore of Naaman shall cleave unto thee, and unto thy seed for ever. And he went out from his presence a leper as white as snow (emphasis added).
> —2 Kings 5:27

In Leviticus, at the 13th chapter, it is explained that black hair was normal among the Hebrews of that day and blonde hair was a sign of a diseased condition.

Leviticus 13 describes how leprosy was diagnosed, how uncleanliness was defined, and how priests tested a person for leprosy. A yellow thin hair was an indication that the person was unclean (Leviticus 13:30, 32).

> Then the priest shall see the plague: and, behold if it be in sight deeper than the skin; and there be in it a yellow thin hair; then the priest shall pronounce him unclean: it is a dry scall, even a leprosy upon the head or beard. (Emphasis added).
> —Leviticus 13:30

A black hair was a sign of good health (Leviticus 13:31, 37).

> But if the stall be in his sight at a stay, and that there is black hair grown up therein: the scall is healed, he is clean: and the priest shall pronounce him clean (emphasis added).
> —Leviticus 13:37

We see then, that among the Afro-Asiatic Hebrews, blonde hair was a sign of a diseased condition, whereas black hair was normal.

(For an excellent discussion by a Black female psychiatrist of the causes of white racism by melanin-deprived persons, see Welsing, *The Isis Papers*).

CHAPTER 17

THE HEBREWS AND THE CANAANITES WERE BOTH PEOPLES OF COLOR AND MERGED INTO ONE ANOTHER

And Abram took Sarai his wife, and Lot his brother's son and all their substance that they had gathered, and the souls that they had gotten in Haran; and they went forth to go into the land of Canaan: and into the land of Canaan they came. And Abram passed through the land unto the place of Sichem, unto the plain of Moreh. And the Canaanite was then in the land (emphasis added).
—Genesis 12;5, 6

As for the Jebusites the inhabitants of Jerusalem, the children of Judah could not drive them out: but the Jebusites dwell with the children of Judah at Jerusalem unto this day.
—Joshua 15:63

THE STORY OF the Hebrews, as told by the Hebrews, themselves, is inextricably intertwined with the Canaanites. The Canaanites and Canaan, the place where Canaanites dwell, are mentioned one hundred and fifty (150) times in the Hebrew Bible.

I: THE HEBREWS WERE WANDERING NOMADS

Whereas I have not dwelt in any house since the time that I brought up the children of Israel out of Egypt, even to this day, but have walked in a <u>tent</u> and in a tabernacle (emphasis added)- 2 Samuel 7:6

"My home has been a <u>*tent*</u>." says the Lord of the wandering <u>A</u>fro-Asiatic tribe that we call the Hebrews.

> And the children of Israel shall pitch their *tents,* every man by his own camp, and every man by his own standard, throughout their hosts (emphasis added).
> —Numbers 1:52

Abraham, the first Hebrew, was told by the Lord to leave his homeland of Mesopotamia in Asia.

> Now the Lord had said unto Abram, Get thee out of thy country, and from thy' kindred, and from thy father's house, unto a land that I will shew thee.
> —*Genesis* 12:1

Abraham was surrounded by people of color, because the Black children of Ham had spread throughout Africa, into the Arabian Peninsula (Yemen, Oman); Iran; Pakistan; and the Indian sub-continent (Genesis 10:6-20).

Abraham wandered from Mesopotamia into the land of Canaan, a land of people of color (Genesis 12:5, 6). From there, he wandered into <u>Africa</u> (Genesis 12:9. 10). While in <u>Africa</u>, his wife Sarah, became a member of the *African* king's <u>harem</u>.

> And it came to pass, that, when Abram was come into Egypt, the Egyptians beheld the woman that she was very fair. The princes also of Pharaoh saw her, and commended her before Pharaoh: and the woman was taken into Pharaoh's house
> -Genesis 12:14, 15

> Then Abram removed his tent and came and dwelt in the plain of Mamre, which is in Hebron, and built there an altar unto the Lord (emphasis added).
>
> —Genesis 13:18

Abraham then wandered back into Canaan. There, he was blessed by Melchizedek, the Canaanite king and priest of Jebus (Salem), the original name of Jerusalem. *(Genesis 14:18-20).*

II: THE HEBREW TENT DWELLERS BECAME CITY DWELLERS IN CANAAN

With the partial conquest of Canaan by Joshua and his descendants, the now Afro-Asiatic Hebrews changed from tent-dwelling nomads to farmers; from pastoral to agricultural life.

> And now the Lord your God hath given rest unto your brethren, as he promised them: therefore now return ye, and get you unto your tents, and unto the land of your procession which Moses the servant of the Lord gave you on the other side of Jordan, So Joshua blessed them, and sent them away; and they went unto their tents. Now to the one half tribe of Manasseh Moses had given possession in Bashan: but unto the other half thereof gave Joshua among- their brethren on this side Jordan westward. And when Joshua sent them away also unto their tent, then he blessed them. And he spake unto them, saying, return with much riches unto your tents, and with very much cattle, with silver, and with gold, and with brass, and with iron, and with very much raiment: divide the spoil of your enemies with your brethren (emphasis added).
>
> -Joshua 22:4, 6-8

They learned from the *Canaanites* in their midst; a cultured and highly civilized nation of agriculturists and city-dwellers.

An article in The New *York Times* credits the ancient inhabitants of Canaan with the invention of agriculture. "That step opened the way to an unprecedented expansion of food supplies and of human population that, in turn, made *cities* and *civilization* possible." The article adds that "The earliest archaeological sites with evidence of domesticated grain lie in the southern Levant, at the north end of the Dead Sea, and date to about 10,000 years ago." *(The* New York *Times*, April 2, 1991, page C-1, column 2).

This is the area centered around *Jericho*, the *city* conquered by Joshua.

> Now Jericho was straitly shut up because of the children of Israel: none went out, and none came in. And the Lord said unto Joshua, See, I have given into thine hand Jericho, and the king thereof, and the mighty men of valour. So the people shouted when the priests blew with the trumpets: and it came to pass, when the people heard the sound of the trumpet, the people shouted with a great shout, that the wall fell down flat, so that the people went up into the *city*, every man straight before him and they took the *city*. And they burnt the *city* with fire, and all that was therein: only the silver, and the gold, and the vessels of brass and of iron, they put into the treasury of the house of the Lord.
> —Joshua 6:1, 2, 20, 24

The *Canaanites* (descendants of *Canaan;* brother of Mizraim, the Egyptian and Cush, the Ethiopian, sons of Ham) were Negroes, already civilized, with whom the nomadic Hebrew tribe later mixed.

> Nevertheless the people be strong that dwell in the land, and the *cities* are walled, and very great: and moreover we saw the children of Anak there. The Amalekites dwell in the land of the south: and the Hittites, and the Jebusites, and

the Amorites, dwell in the mountains: and the Canaanites dwell by the sea, and by the coast of Jordan.

—Numbers 13:28,29

The invading Israelite Bedouins took over a heritage from their agricultural predecessors in Palestine.

And I have given you a land for which ye did not labour, and <u>cities</u> which ye built not, and ye dwell in them; of the vineyards and oliveyards which ye planted not do ye eat. (emphasis added).

—Joshua 24:13

III: THE CANAANITE INFLUENCE UPON THEIR HEBREW COUSINS

And the children of Israel dwelt among the <u>Canaanites</u>, Hittites, and Amorites, and Perizzites, and Hivites, and Jebusites: And they took their daughters to their wives, and gave their daughters to their sons and served their gods (emphasis added).

—Judges 3:5, 6

After the partial conquest of Canaan, the invading, nomadic <u>tent</u>-dwelling <u>Afro</u>-Asiatic Hebrew tribes and the black city-dwelling Canaanite agricultural tribes lived together (Joshua 13:2-6). Each one's sons married the other one's daughters. Not only did the Hebrew tribes live side by side with the Canaanites, but, in the end, the two peoples merged into each other (Judges 1:21, 27-35).

And it came to pass, when Israel was strong that they put the Canaanites to tribute, and did not utterly drive them out.

- Judges 1:28

Abraham married a _Canaanite_ woman.

> Then again Abraham took a wife, and her name was Keturah.
> — Genesis 25:1

His third wife, Keturah, must have been a _Canaanite_ for the following reasons:

1. After his death, she was called a concubine, not a wife (Genesis 25:6).
2. Her children did not inherit (Genesis 25:6).

> But unto the sons of the concubines, which Abraham had, Abraham gave gifts, and sent them away from Isaac his son, while he yet lived, eastward, unto the east country.
> —Genesis 25:6 3.

3. Her son by Abraham, Shuah, whose father was the original Hebrew, was a <u>Canaanite</u>.
   And Judah saw there a daughter of a certain Canaanite whose name was Shuah; and he took her and went in unto her. —Genesis 38:2

Since Shuah obviously did not become a _Canaanite_ through his father, who was a Hebrew, it must have come about through the matriarchal system of Black cultures whereby the children belong to the mother's clan.

> Abraham and Sarah both died in and were buried in the Land of <u>Canaan</u>
> (Genesis 23:19, 25:8-10).

> And after this, Abraham buried Sarah his wife in the cave of the field of Machpelah before Mamre: the same is Hebron in the land of' Canaan.
> - Genesis 23:19

Their son Isaac, second patriarch of the House of Israel, was born and died in the land of Canaan (Genesis 21:2, 3; 35:27-29).

Jacob, third patriarch of Israel, and the father of the twelve tribes of Israel, was also born in the land of Canaan (Genesis 25:26). He resided in Canaan (Genesis 33:18; 37:1) and was buried in Canaan (Genesis 50:13).

> And Jacob dwelt in the land wherein his father was a stranger, in the land of Canaan.(emphasis added)
> —Genesis 37:1

> And when Jacob had made an end of commanding his sons, he gathered up his feet into the bed and yielded up the ghost, and was gathered unto his people.
> —Genesis 49:33

> For his sons carried him into the land of Canaan, and buried him in the cave of the field of Machpelah, which Abraham brought with the field for a possession of a burying place of Ephron the Hittite, before Mamre.(emphasis added)
> —Genesis 50:13

Joseph was reburied in Canaan (Joshua 24:32). His brother, Judah, founder of the tribe of Judah, one of the twelve tribes of Israel, married a Canaanite woman.

> And in process of time the daughter of Shuah Judah's wife died: and Judah was comforted, and went up unto his sheepshearers to Timnath, he and his friend Hirah the Adullamite
> —Genesis 38:12

Judah's Canaanite wife, the mother of the tribe of Judah, was the daughter of Shuah, Abraham's son by his third wife, Keturah (Genesis 25:2). Judah's children by the *Canaanite* daughter of Shuah were named Er, Onan, and

Shelah (Genesis 38:1-5). It was the tribe of Judah, which later had the honor of conquering Jebus (Salem) (Judges 1:8)

> Now the children of Judah had fought against Jerusalem, and had taken it, and smitten it with the edge of the sword, and set the city on fire.
>
> —Judges 1:8

IV: THE BATTLE FOR THE LAND OF CANAAN WAS A SEE-SAW AFFAIR, IN WHICH FIRST ONE SIDE PREVAILED FOR A TIME, THEN THE OTHER SIDE PREVAILED

> Therefore the anger of the Lord was hot against Israel and he sold them into the hand of Chushanrishathaiim king of Mesopotamia: and the children of Israel served Chushanrishathaim eight years. So the children of Israel served Eglon the king Moab eighteen years.
>
> —Judges 5:8, 14

At its peak, the Egyptian Empire controlled the land of Canaan. The Canaanites paid annual tribute to the Egyptian king. The Prophet Isaiah predicted that, once again, there would be a highway stretching from Egypt (through Canaan) to Assyria (Iraq).

> In that day shall there be a highway out of Egypt to Assyria, and the Assyrian shall come into Egypt, and the Egyptians shall serve with the Assyrians.
>
> —Isaiah 19:23

There is a record of the Canaanites petitioning the Egyptians for help against the invaders (called by them "Habiru"). With the decline of Egyptian power and influence (similar to that of Rome), the response was fitful and unavailing. But, there was a response.

Shishak, King of Egypt, laid waste to Judah, sacked Jerusalem, and took all of Solomon's treasures back to Egypt with him (2 Chronicles 12:9).

> So Shishak king of Egypt came up against Jerusalem, and took away the treasures of the house of the Lord, and the treasures of the king's house; he took all: he carried away also the shields of gold which Solomon had made.
> —2 Chronicles 12:9

The Ethiopian general, Zerah, later came with one million black troops, but was repulsed by King Asa at Mareshah. -2 Chronicles 14:9.

> And there came out against them Zerah the Ethiopian with a host of a thousand thousand and three hundred chariots: and came unto Mareshah.
> —2 Chronicles 14:9

(A million Blacks in ONE bible verse!)

As the Hebrews prevailed and rested upon their laurels, they forgot the admonitions of their prophets and leaders, fell away from their God, and began worshipping the gods of the Canaanites living among them
-Judges 3:7, 8:34, and 10:6

> And it came to pass, as soon as Gideon was dead, that the children of Israel turned again, and went a whoring after Baalim and made Baalberith their god.
> —Judges 8:33

In turn, the Lord frequently punished them by allowing their enemies to conquer them, thus reminding them of their need to worship the Lord alone and not false idols. The Hebrews were enslaved several times after the death of Joshua because they worshipped false gods *(Judges,* chapters three and four).

> And the children of Israel did evil in the sight of the Lord: and the Lord delivered them into the hand of Midian seven years.
> —Judges 6:1

During **this** entire time, the Canaanites were living side-by-side with the Hebrews, intermarrying and having children by each other (Joshua 13:13; 16:10; 17:12: Judges 1:27-35).

> And the children of Benjamin did not drive out the Jebusites that inhabited Jerusalem; but the Jebusites dwell with the children of Benjamin in Jerusalem unto this day.
> —Judges 1:21

V: MANY HEBREW LEADERS WERE OF CANAANITE DESCENT.

> And Gideon had three score and ten sons of his body begotten: for he had many wives. And his concubine that was in Shechem, she also bare him a son, whose name he called Abimelech.
> —Judges 8:30, 31

Gideon, who saved Israel with his 300 soldiers, was descended from Joseph and his African wife, Asenath, through their son, Manasseh (Judges 6:15).

> And he said unto him, Oh my Lord, wherewith shall I save Israel? behold, my family is poor in Manasseh, and I am the least in my father's house.
> --Judges 6:15

King Abimelech was the son of Gideon by a non-Hebrew woman (concubine), and he could not inherit from his father (Judges 8:31). He made himself king by force of arms, with the help of his mother's people (the Canaanites) (Judges 9:1-6).

> And his concubine that was in Shechem, she also bare him a son, whose name he called Abimelech.
> —Judges 8:31

> And all the men of Shechem gathered together, and all the house of Millo, and went, and made Abimelech king, by the plain of the pillar that was in Shechem.
> —Judges 9:6

Caleb, a leader of the tribe of Judah, received a large land grant in the promised land from Joshua for his valiant work as a Hebrew scout in the Canaanite land (Joshua 14:6-15; 15:13-19). Caleb and the entire tribe of Judah were descended from a Canaanite mother (Genesis 38:1-5).

> Hebron therefore became the inheritance of Caleb the son of Jephunneh the Kenezite unto this day, because that he wholly followed the Lord God of Israel.
> —Joshua 14:14

The great hero, *Joshua*, who led the Hebrews into the Promised Land, was of *African* descent. He was from the tribe of Ephraim (Numbers 13:8, 16). The mother of Ephraim and the mother of the tribe of Ephraim was an *African* woman named Asenath (Genesis 41:45-52).

Jephthah, a judge of Israel, was the son of Gilead by a non-Hebrew woman (harlot) and could not inherit (Judges, chapter 11). He became *Judge* of Israel by his successful defense of the Hebrews against the Amorites/Ammonites (Canaanites) (Judges, chapter 12).

Ibzan, Judge of Israel, had thirty sons and thirty daughters, all of whom married non-Hebrews (Judges 12:8-10).

One *of* the twelve disciples of Jesus Christ was *Simon* the <u>Canaanite</u>! (Mark 3:18). Jesus had no Greek or Roman disciples. (See Jacobs, *The Hebrew Heritage of Black Africa-Fully Documented.*)

> Now the names of the twelve apostles are these: the first, Simon, who is called Peter, and Andrew his brother; James the son of Zebedee, and John his brother; Philip, and Bartholomew; Thomas, and Matthew the publican; James the son of Alphaeus and Labbaeus, whose surname was Thaddaeus; Simon the <u>Canaanite</u>, And Judas Iscariot, who also betrayed him (emphasis added).
>
> —Matthew 10:2-4

Truly, the Last Supper was a Black experience! Read on for further proofs.

CHAPTER 18

BLACK AND BEAUTIFUL IN KING SOLOMON'S HAREM

And Solomon made affinity with Pharaoh king of Egypt, and took <u>Pharaoh's daughter</u>, and brought her into the city of David, until he had made an end of building his own house, and the house of the LORD, and the wall of Jerusalem round about (emphasis added).

— 1 Kings 3:1

I. SOLOMON, THE RICHEST AND WISEST MAN IN THE ANCIENT WORLD, TAKES A BLACK BRIDE

KING SOLOMON, THE wisest man in the ancient world, married an *African* princess. He sealed his alliance with the Black king of Egypt by marrying the king's daughter and bringing her to Jebus (Salem), now the City of David (Jerusalem).

The African King of Egypt then fulfilled his part of the bargain by sending an army to conquer the *Canaanite* city of Gezer and by giving the city to his daughter as a dowry present.

> For Pharaoh king of Egypt had gone up, and taken Gezer, and burnt it with fire, and slain the Canaanites that dwelt in the city, and given it for a present unto his daughter, Solomon's wife.
>
> - 1Kings 9:16

Solomon rebuilt the city and moved his African wife into the new palace he had built for her.

> But Pharaoh's daughter came up out of the city of David unto her house which Solomon had built for her: then did he build Millo.
>
> —1 Kings 9:24

II. SOLOMON LOVES MANY BLACK WOMEN

> But King Solomon loved many strange women, together with the daughter of Pharaoh, women of the Moabites, Ammonites, Edomites, Zidonians, and Hittites: And he had seven hundred wives, princesses, and three hundred concubines: and his wives turned away his heart.
>
> —1 Kings 11:1,3

Not content with marrying an *African* princess, Solomon married many other (*Canaanite*) women of color. He married Hittite women, Edomite women, Zidonian women, and Moabite women. He had a total of one thousand wives and concubines in his harem.

III. A VOICE SPEAKS FROM SOLOMON'S BLACK HAREM

> I am <u>*Black*</u>, but comely, O ye daughters of Jerusalem, as the tents of Kedar, as the curtains of Solomon (emphasis added).
> —Song of Solomon 1:5

> Look not upon me, because I am <u>*Black*</u>, because the sun hath looked upon me: my mother's children were angry with me; they made me the keeper of the vineyards; but mine own vineyard have I not kept (emphasis added)
> —Song of Solomon 1:6

Solomon was the richest and wisest man in the ancient world.

> So King Solomon exceeded all the kings of the earth for riches and for wisdom. And all the earth sought to Solomon, to hear his wisdom, which God had put in his heart.
> —1 kings 10:23, 24

Yet, he found time to write poetry. In his famous love poem, known as the Song of Solomon, one of the new members of his harem described herself as being Black, black as the tents of *Kedar*.

Kedar was an Arab; the grandson of Abraham and Abraham's *African* wife, Hagar, through their son Ishmael, the first Arab.

> And these are the names of the sons of Ishmael, by their names, according to their generations: the firstborn of

Ishmael, Nebajoth: and *Kedar,* and Adbeel, and Mibsam (emphasis added).
—Genesis 25:13

Kedar, a Black son of Ishmael, and his tribe are mentioned eleven times in the Bible.

Solomon's black bride asks the ladies of Jebus (Salem) not to look down upon her because of her complexion. Solomon tells her again and again she is beautiful.

If thou know not, O thou fairest among women, go thy way forth among women, go thy way forth by the footsteps of the flock, and feed thy kids beside the shepherds' tents.
—Song of Solomon 1:8

Behold, thou art fair, my love: behold, thou art fair; thou hast dove's eyes within thy locks: thy hair is as a flock of goats that appear from mount Gilead.
—Song of Solomon 4:1

Thou art beautiful, 0 my love, as Tirzah, comely as Jerusalem, terrible as an army with banners.
—Song of Solomon 6:4

CHAPTER 19

FIVE MORE BIBLICAL REASONS WHY THE EARLY HEBREWS WERE A PEOPLE OF COLOR

> I beheld till the thrones were cast down, and the Ancient of Days did sit, whose garment was white as snow, and the hair of his head like the pure <u>wool</u>; his throne was like the fiery flame, and his wheels as burning fire (emphasis added).
> —Daniel 7:9

1. THE GOD OF THE HEBREWS WAS BLACK

GENESIS TELLS US that God created man in his own image.

> So God created man in his own image, in the image of God created he him; male and female he created them.
> —Genesis 1:27

The prophet Daniel at Daniel 7:9 describes a vision in which he saw his God (the Ancient of Days). Daniel viewed his God as a woolly haired Black man. Daniel describes the Ancient of Days as wearing a garment as white as snow with the hair of his head like pure wool. Of all the races of man, the only one whose hair is woolly is the Black race. Thus, the God of the Hebrews was a woolly haired Black man.

Going further in the Book of Daniel, another great vision is described. At Daniel 10:5, 6, Daniel sees a vision of someone whose arms and feet were the color of polished *brass*. Clearly, he saw his great vision as a person of color.

> Then I lifted up mine eyes and looked, and behold a certain man clothed in linen, whose loins were girded with fine gold of Uphaz: His body also was like the beryl, and his face as the appearance of lightning, and his eyes as lamps of fire, and his arms and his feet like in colour to polished brass, and the voice of his words like the voice of a multitude.
> —Daniel 10:5, 6

2. BLACK EGYPTIANS ACCOMPANIED THE HEBREWS OUT OF EGYPT

> Thou shalt not abhor an Edomite; for he is thy brother: thou shalt not abhor an Egyptian; because thou wast a stranger in his land. The children that are begotten of them shall enter into the congregation of the Lord in their third generation.
> —Deuteronomy 23:7, 8

The fifth book of Moses instructs the Afro-Asiatic Hebrew tribe not to abhor the Egyptians (*Africans*) in their midst. The children of the inter-marriages between pure *Africans* (Egyptians) and Afro-Asiatic Hebrews are to be eligible to enter into the congregation of the Lord in the third generation. Thus, there were black Egyptians among the Hebrews.

3. JERUSALEM WAS CONQUERED BY BLACK EGYPT

> And it came to pass in the fifth year of King Rehoboam, that Shishak king of Egypt came up against Jerusalem.
> —1 Kings 14:25

During the fifth year of the reign of King Rehoboam, Shishak, King of Egypt, conquered Jerusalem, despoiled the temple, took away the measures of the house of the Lord and the treasures of the king's house and all that he surveyed. Shishak took away all the shields of gold that Solomon had made (1 Kings 14:25, 26). When Black Egypt conquered Jerusalem, the capital city of the Hebrews, everything was taken. Of course, conquering soldiers have been known to have children by the women of the people they conquered. The children resulting from Egypt's rampage over Jerusalem would have the blood of the black Egyptian soldiers and would carry the outward appearance of the soldiers as well.

> And he took away the treasures of the house of the Lord, and the treasures of the king's house; he even took away all: he took away all the shields of gold which Solomon had made.
> —1 Kings 14:26.

4. THE MASS INTERMARRIAGE OF HEBREWS WITH OTHER PEOPLES OF COLOR WAS A SOURCE OF COMMUNITY CONCERN

> And Shechaniah the son of Jehiel, one of the sons of Elam, answered and said unto Ezra, We have trespassed against our God, and have taken *strange wives* of the people of the land: yet now there is hope in Israel concerning this thing.
> —Ezra 10:2

The chief priest of the Hebrews, Ezra, deplored the mixed marriages and then dissolved them (Ezra 9:1). Ezra claimed that the Hebrews had not separated themselves from the people of the lands, including the Canaanites, the Hittites, Perizzites, the Jebusites, the Amorites, the Moabires, and the Egyptians. We know from the earlier books of the Bible that the Canaanites, the Egyptians, and the Amorites were people of color.

At Ezra 9:2, the chief priest Ezra observes that the Hebrews have taken the daughters of the peoples of color for themselves and for their sons. Ezra laments that the holy seed of the Hebrews has mingled itself with the people of those lands. Ezra goes so far as to say that the rulers and princes of the Hebrews have been foremost in this trespass. Ezra describes himself as being so upset about the intermarriage and intermingling of Hebrews with other peoples of the land that he tore his garment and cut the hair off his head and beard.

Finally, Ezra lists all the Hebrews who have taken strange wives, including the sons of priests (Ezra 10:18-44). In Ezra's eyes, we have a contemporary observer of the ancient Hebrews and their affairs. Certainly, we can rely on Ezra's observation that there was a tremendous amount of intermarriage between Hebrews and the surrounding peoples, many of whom were people of color.

> And Ezra the priest stood up, and said unto them, Ye have transgressed, and have taken strange wives to increase the trespass of Israel. Now therefore make confession unto the Lord God of your fathers, and do his pleasure: and separate yourselves from the people of the land, and from the strange wives.
> —Ezra 10:10, 11.

5. THE HEBREWS LIVED AND CONTINUED TO LIVE IN AFRICAN NATIONS OF COLOR EVEN AFTER THEY ESCAPED FROM EGYPTIAN BONDAGE

> "The word that came to Jeremiah concerning all the Jews which dwell in the land of Egypt, which dwell at Migdol, and at Tahpanhes, and at Noph, and in the country of Pathros, saying,"
> —Jeremiah 44:1

Hebrews lived in Black Egypt, Black Sudan, and other African countries of color and continued to live in these settings even after their escape from bondage.

CHAPTER 20

THE LOST TRIBES OF ISRAEL-FOUND IN AFRICA

> And he rose and went; and behold, a man of *Ethiopia*, an eunuch of great authority under Candace queen of the *Ethiopians*, who had the charge of all her treasure, and had come to Jerusalem for to worship (emphasis added).
> —Acts 8:27

> And it shall come to pass in that day, that the Lord shall set his hand again the second time to recover the remnant of his people, which shall be left from Assyria, and from <u>Egypt</u>, and from <u>Pathros</u>, and from <u>Cush</u>, and from Elam, and from Shinar, and from Hamath, and from the islands of the sea (emphasis added).
> —Isaiah 11:11

> Princes shall come out of *Egypt; Ethiopia* shall soon stretch out her hands unto God. (emphasis added).
> —Psalms 68:31

THE TWELVE TRIBES of Israel are today scattered abroad, including into *African* countries. The Bible proves this. Zephaniah predicts the scattering of Hebrews into *Africa* by stating that the dispersed Hebrews shall bring an offering unto the Lord from beyond the rivers of Ethiopia.

> "From beyond the rivers of Ethiopia my suppliants, even the daughter of my dispersed, shall bring mine offering (emphasis added)."
>
> —Zephaniah 3:10

This suggests that at least a remnant of the Hebrews will reside beyond the rivers of *Ethiopia*, a black nation. Indeed, Ms. Israel 2013, Yityish Aynaw, was born in Ethiopia!

It is interesting to note that the prophet Zephaniah was probably a person of color. He is listed as the son of Cushi.

> "The word of the Lord which came unto Zephaniah the son of Cushi, the son of Gedaliah, the son of Amariah, the son of Hizkiah, in the days of Josiah, the son of Amon, king of Judah."
>
> -Zephaniah 1:1

The name "Cushi" in the Bible usually signifies *an African,* a man from Cush (2 Samuel 18:21-32).

> Then said Joab to Cushi, Go tell the king what thou has seen, And Cushi bowed himself unto Joab, and ran.
> —2 Samuel 18:21

The Prince of Prophets, Isaiah, predicted that a remnant of Israel would return one day from Assyria, Egypt, Pathros, Cush, Elam, Shinar, and Hamath (Isaiah 11:11). Cush is black Ethiopia. Pathros is black Sudan, Egypt is black Egypt (Bleiberg, Jewish Life in Ancient Egypt). Isaiah also predicted that one day, five cities in the land of Egypt would speak the language of Canaan; that is, five cities of black Egypt would speak Hebrew (Isaiah 19:18).

Another prophet predicted that the Lord would sift the House of Israel among all nations as corn is sifted in a sieve.

> "For, lo, I will command, and I will sift the house of Israel among all nations, like as corn is sifted in a sieve. yet shall not the least grain fall upon the earth."
>
> —Amos 9:9

In the Book of Acts, a Black Jew, the eunuch from Ethiopia, came to Jerusalem to worship, because he was a Hebrew. While there, he met with the Evangelist Philip, who converted him to Christianity and baptized him. This is a biblical example of an African Hebrew —a person of color—from Ethiopia— coming to Jerusalem and being converted to Christianity. And indeed, there are many Christians in Ethiopia today. Again, we see how the prophecies and stories contained in the Bible are confirmed by today's headlines.

> And he rose and went: and, behold, a man of Ethiopia. an eunuch of great authority under Candace queen of Ethiopians, who had charge of all her treasure, and had come to Jerusalem for to worship, was returning, and sitting in his chariot read Esaias the prophet. Then the spirit said unto Philip, Go near, and join thyself to this chariot. Then Philip opened his mouth, and began at the same scripture and preached unto him Jesus.
>
> —Acts 8:27-29, 35.

Finally, the Book of James begins with a greeting to the twelve tribes that are scattered abroad, indicating that the Hebrews had been scattered all over the earth as prophesied in earlier biblical writings. (See Koestler, The Thirteenth Tribe.)

> James, a servant of God and of the Lord Jesus Christ. to the twelve tribes which are scattered abroad, greeting.
>
> —James 1:1

CHAPTER 21

TWO BROWN QUEENS IN THE NEW TESTAMENT

> And he arose and went, and, behold, a man of *Ethiopia*. an eunuch of great authority under Candace *queen* of the *Ethiopians,*, who had the charge of all her treasure, and had come to Jerusalem for to worship (emphasis added).
>
> — Acts 8:27

> The *queen of the south* shall *rise* up in the judgment with this generation, and shall condemn it: for *She* came from the uttermost parts of the earth to hear the wisdom of Solomon: and, behold, a greater than Solomon is here (emphasis added).
>
> —Matthew 12:42

THE BOOK OF Acts, in telling the story of the conversion to Christianity of the Ethiopian eunuch by the apostle Philip, informs us that the eunuch was under the authority of a queen named Candace (Acts 8:27).

(See Andrews, *Bible Legacy of the Black Race*.)

Ethiopia, in the Bible, was the land south of Egypt. It was named by the Greeks the land of sunburned faces (Aithiops). Candace was a black queen.

Sheba was the son of Raamah, and the grandson of Cush (Ethiopia) (Genesis 10:7). The name Sheba also refers to a region in southwestern Arabia.

> And the sons of Cush, Seba and Havilah, and Sabtah, and Raamah, and Sabtechah: and the sons of Raamah, Sheba, and Dedan.
>
> —Genesis 10:7

The original Arabs of southern Arabia (Yemen) were a Black race, closely related to the Ethiopians. They later established a dynasty, known as the Abbasids, which conquered the world, from the Indus River (India) to the Atlantic Ocean. Known as the Moors, they ruled substantial parts of Europe from their capital in Baghdad (Iraq). When they finally retreated from Spain back to Africa, after six hundred years of dominance, they left behind traces of their long stay in the dark hair, dark eyes and dark skins of the Spanish people.

The New Testament twice mentions the visit of the Queen of Sheba to Solomon, King of the Hebrews (Matthew 12:42 and Luke 11:31). The story of the visit of the Queen of Sheba to King Solomon is told in greater detail in the Old Testament (I Kings 10; 1-10; II Chronicles 9: I -12).

> And when the queen of Sheba heard of the fame of Solomon concerning the name of the Lord, she came to prove him with hard questions.
>
> — Kings 10:1

QUEEN OF SHEBA

CHAPTER 22

BLACK PROPHETS OF THE EARLY CHRISTIAN CHURCH

Now there were in the church that was at Antioch certain prophets and teachers; as Barnabas, and Simeon that was called *Niger*, and Lucius of *Cyrene* and Manaen, which had been brought up with Herod the Tetrarch and Saul (emphasis added).

—Acts 13:1

And some of them were men of Cyprus and *Cyrene*, which, when they were come to Antioch spake unto the Grecians, preaching the Lord Jesus (emphasis added).

—Acts 11:20

And there were dwelling at Jerusalem Jews, devout men, out of every nation under heaven.

—Acts 2:5

THE CHRISTIAN CHURCH was born on the Day of Pentecost. On that glorious day of Pentecost, the disciples, apostles, and believers began speaking in tongues.

And they were all filled with the Holy Ghost, and began to speak with other tongues, as the Spirit gave them utterance.

—Acts 2:4

Who was there when the Church of Jesus Christ was born?

The Scripture reports that **Africans** were present, people from Egypt and Libya (both *African* nations) (Acts 2:10).

> And how hear we every man in our own tongue, wherein we were born? Parthians, and Medes, and Elamites, and the dwellers in Mesopotamia, and in Judaea, and Cappadocia in Pontus, and Asia, Phrygia, and Pamphylia in Egypt, and in the parts of Libya about Cyrene, and strangers of Rome, Jews and proselytes, Cretes and Arabians, we do hear them speak in our tongues the wonderful works of God.(emphasis added)
> —Acts 2:8-11

Asia was represented by Parthians (inhabitants of Parthia, now Iran); Medes (inhabitants of Media, a country north of Persia); Elamites (foreign (Persian) settlers in Samaria); dwellers in Mesopotamia (the Asian land between the Tigris and Euphrates rivers); Cappadocia (a Roman province in Asia minor); Pontus (a Roman province in Asia Minor); Phrygia (a Roman province in Asia Minor); Pamphylia (a province of Asia Minor) (Acts 2:9, 10).

There were also present Arabians (inhabitants of the northern part of the Arabian peninsula), dwellers in Judea (a Roman province), and Cretes (inhabitants of Crete, an island south of Greece) (Acts 2:9-11).

Europeans ("*Strangers* of Rome") were noted as being **visitors** among the black and brown Africans and Asians who predominated on this great occasion (Acts 2:10).

Later, we find *African* believers (men of Cyrene, an *African* city) preaching Jesus to the idol-worshipping, European pagans (Grecians) (Acts 11:20). (See Otabil, *Beyond the Rivers* of Ethiopia.)

> And some of them were men of Cyprus and Cyrene, which, when they were come to Antioch, spake unto the Grecians, preaching the Lord Jesus.
> —Acts 11:20

The Scripture reports that *African* preachers, missionaries, and teachers converted many of the idol-worshipping *European Pagans.* (Acts 11:21).

> And some of them were men of Cyprus and Cyrene which, when they were come to Antioch, spake unto the Grecians, preaching the Lord Jesus. And the hand of the Lord was with them: and a great number believed, and turned unto the Lord.
> —Acts 11:20, 21

It was at Antioch (a city of Syria), where we were first called Christians.

> And the disciples were called Christians first in Antioch.
> —Acts 11:26

Among the prophets at Antioch were Simeon, also called the black man (Niger), and the *African* from Cyrene named Lucius (Acts 13:1), who may be Doctor Luke, the author of the Gospel of Luke.

> Timotheus my workfellow, and Lucius, and Jason, and Sosipater, my kinsmen, salute you.
> — Romans 16:21

> Luke, the beloved physician,Demas, greet you.
> —Colossians 4:14

> Only Luke is with me. Take Mark, and bring him with thee for he is profitable to me for the ministry.
> —2 Timothy 4:11

SIMEON (NIGER)

CHAPTER 23

SIMON THE AFRICAN CARRIED THE CROSS FOR JESUS CHRIST

> And as they came out, they found a man of Cyrene, Simon by name: him they compelled to bear his cross.
> —Matthew 27:32

WHEN JESUS WAS on his way to be crucified, he *was* so weak that he was unable **to** carry his own cross. Therefore, a man named Simon was compelled to bear the cross for Jesus. The Bible states that Simon was a man of Cyrene, which is an ancient city in north *Africa* in what is now the nation of Libya.

Therefore, the man who carried the cross for Jesus was an *African*. This account is repeated in the gospels of Mark and Luke (Mark 15:21, Luke 23:26).

> And they compel one Simon a Cyrenian, who passed by, coming out of the country, the father of Alexander and Rufus, to bear his cross.
> —Mark 15:21

> And as they **led** him away, they laid hold upon one Simon, a Cyrenian, coming out of the country, and on him they laid the cross that he might bear it after Jesus.
> — Luke 23:26

Mark goes on to describe Simon as the father of Alexander and Rufus. We later find Simon's son, Rufus, named as a notable Christian (Romans 16:13).

> Salute Rufus chosen in the Lord, and his mother and mine.
> — Romans 16:13

CHAPTER 24

JESUS WAS BLACK

And in the midst of the seven candlesticks, one like unto the Son of man, clothed with a garment down to the foot, and girt about the paps with a golden girdle. His head and his hairs were white like <u>wool</u>, as white as snow; and his eyes were as a flame of fire; And his feet like unto fine brass, as if they <u>burned</u> in a furnace; and his voice as the sound of many waters (emphasis added).

—Revelation 1:13-15

> For unto us a child is born, unto us a son is given: and the government shall be upon his shoulder: and his name shall be called Wonderful, Counsellor, The mighty God, The everlasting Father, The prince of Peace.
>
> — Isaiah 9:6

JESUS WAS PREDICTED in the Old Testament by, among others, the prophet Isaiah (Isaiah 9:6). The composer Handel later used Isaiah's language in his famous musical work known as *The Messiah*. The words describe none other than Jesus Christ.

As predicted in the Old Testament, Jesus did come. When He came, He was a Hebrew. As a Hebrew, He had to be a person of color, because the <u>Afro</u>-Asiatic Hebrews were a people of color.

When King Herod wanted to kill the young Jesus, Joseph and Mary took Jesus to hide in <u>Africa</u>, where he would not stand out! After all, the ancient Egyptians were Black! (See chapter 4).

> "And when they were departed, behold, the angel of the Lord appeareth to Joseph in a dream, saying, Arise, and take the young child and his mother, and flee into Egypt, and be thou there until I bring thee word: for Herod will seek the young child to destroy him."
>
> —Matthew 2:13

The New Testament specifically begins where the Old Testament leaves off. The Old Testament is completed with the Book of Malachi —the end of the Hebrew prophets. The very next words in the Bible are -The book of the generation of Jesus Christ, the son of David, the son of Abraham" (Matthew 1:1). Thus, we are told from the very beginning *of* the New Testament that Jesus is a direct descendant of David and Abraham, both of whom were people of color. Both of them were Semites. Both of them *were* Hebrews. Jesus Christ is in that tradition, in that direct line of descent.

Not only was He a Hebrew, but He was a religious Hebrew. He was a rabbi.

> Nathanael answered and saith unto him, "Rabbi, thou art the Son of God' thou art the King of Israel.
> —John 1:49

Later we find him going up to Jerusalem, the city of David (formerly Jebus/Salem, the city of Melchizedek) to celebrate the Passover.

> And the Jews Passover was at hand, and Jesus went up to Jerusalem.
> —John 2:13

Pontius Pilate called him "Jesus of Nazareth— King of the Jews" (John 19:19-22). When the chief priests of the Hebrews learned of this, they went to Pilate complaining, stating that he was not the king of the Jews, but that he *said* he was king of the Jews. Pilate answered them, "What I have written, I have written."

> And Pilate wrote a title, and put it on the cross. And the writing was, JESUS OF NAZARETH, THE KING OF THE JEWS.
> —John 19:19

The Book of Revelation states that Jesus Christ, in his own words, is "the root and offspring of David"

> Jesus has sent mine angel to testify unto you these things in the churches. I am the root and the offspring of David, and the bright and morning star.
> —Revelation 22:16

Jesus was clearly a Hebrew. If the Hebrews were a people of color, then Jesus was a person of color. (See Mosley, *What Color Was Jesus?*)

The Book of Revelation was written by St. John the Divine, who was one of the disciples of Jesus Christ. Indeed, John was the favorite disciple of Jesus

Christ and sat on his right hand at the Last Supper. John walked with Jesus when Jesus was a young Black man in Palestine. John knew what Jesus looked like.

In chapter 1, John gives us his vision of a glorified Christ. He tells us, beginning at verse 10 of the first chapter, that he was in the spirit on the Lord's Day, and he heard a great voice as of a trumpet. At verse 12, he turns to see the voice that spoke with him. At verse 13, he sees someone who looks like the Son of Man —Jesus—completely covered up except for the head and the feet. What did the head look like? At verse 14, we find that the hairs were white like wool. In verse 15, we learn that the feet were like fine *brass* as if they *burned* in a furnace. John is describing someone—his Jesus—as having hair that was woolly, and feet that looked as if they had been burned in a furnace. He was describing a Black man.

> His head and his hairs were white like <u>wool</u>, as white as snow: and his eyes were as a flame of fire. And his feet like unto fine <u>brass</u>, as if they <u>burned</u> in a furnace: and his voice as the sound of many waters (emphasis added).
>
> Revelation 1:14, 15

JESUS THE CHRIST

SELECTED BIBLIOGRAPHY

African Presence in Early Asia, New Brunswick, New *Jersey*: Edited by Ivan Van Sertima and Runoko Rashidi: Transaction Publishers, 1988.

Aharoni, Yohanan, and AviYonah, Michael. The Macmillan *Bible Atlas*, New York: MacMillan Publishing Company, 1968.

Andrews, Joyce. *Bible Legacy of the Black Race*, Nashville, Tennessee: Winston-Derek Publishers, Inc., 1993.

Bernal. Martin. *Black Athena --The Afro-Asiatic Roots of Classical Civilization*, Vol. 1, New Brunswick, New Jersey: Rutgers University Press, 1987.

Bleiberg, Edward. *Jewish Life In Ancient Egypt*, Brooklyn, New York: Brooklyn Museum of Art, 2002.

Boyd, Paul C. *The African Origin of Christianity*, London, United Kingdom: Karia Press, 1991.

Cline, Eric *From Eden to Exile*, Washington, D.C.: National Geographic. 2007.

Copher, Charles B. *"Blacks and Jews in Historical Interaction: The Biblical-African Experience,"* Journal of the Interdenominational Theological Center. Vol. Ill, Number 1, Fall 1975, Pages 9-16.

Darkwah, Nana Banchie. *The Africans* Who Wrote *the Bible*, Russellville, AR, 2002.

Diop, Cheikh Anta. *The African Origin of Civilization*, Chicago, Illinois: Lawrence Hill 13:13 PM Co., 1974.

—— *Civilization or Barbarism*, Chicago, Illinois: Lawrence Hill Books, 1991.

Dunston, Alfred G. *The Black Man in The Old Testament and His World*, Trenton, New Jersey: Africa World Press, Inc., 1992.

Felder, Cain Hope. *Troubling Biblical Waters*, Matthew Knoll, New York: Orbis Books, 1989.

Freud, Sigmund. *Moses and Monotheism*, New York, New York: Vintage Books, 1939

Jackson, John C. *Christianity Before Christ*, Austin, Texas: American Atheist Press, 1985.

—— *Ethiopia and the Origin of Civilization*, Baltimore, Maryland: Black Classic Press, 1939.

Jacobs, Steven S. *The Hebrew Heritage of Black Africa* , Brooklyn. New York: Monami Publications. 1976.

James, George G.M. *Stolen Legacy*, San Francisco, California: Julian Richardson Associates, 1954.

Johnson, John L. *The Black Bible Heritage*, Nashville, Tennessee: Winston-Derek Publishers, Inc., 1975.

Koestler, Arthur. *The Thirteenth Tribe*, New York, New York: Popular Library, 1976.

McCray, Rev. Walter Arthur. The *Black Presence in the Bible*, Chicago, Illinois: Black Light Fellowship. 1990.

Mears, Henrietta C. *What the Bible is all About*, Ventura, California: Regal Books,1953.

Morrisey, Richard A. *Bible History of the Negro*, Nashville, Tennessee: National Baptist Publishing Board, 1925.

—— *Colored People in Bible History*, Hammond, Indiana: W.B. Conkey, CO., 1925.

Mosley, William. *What Color* Was *Jesus*? Chicago, Illinois: African American Images, 1987.

The New *Strong's Concordance of the Bible*, Nashville, Tennessee: Thomas Nelson, Inc., 1985.

Otabil, Mensa. *Beyond the Rivers of Ethiopia*, Lanham, Maryland: Pneuma Life Publishing, 1993.

Parker, George Wells. *The Children of the Sun*, Baltimore, Maryland: Black Classic Press, 1918.

Peterson, Carlisle John. *The Destiny of the Black Race*, Toronto, Canada: Lifeline Communications, 1991.

The Story of the Bible, New York: William Wise & Co., 1939.

Welsing, Frances Cress. *The Isis Papers, Chicago*, Illinois: Third World Press, 1991.

Williams, Chancellor. *The Destruction of Black Civilization*, Chicago, Illinois: Third World Press, 1987.

Windsor, Rudolph R. *From Babylon to Timbuktu*, Smithtown, New York: Exposition Press, 1969.

The Wycliffe Bible Commentary, Chicago, Illinois: Editors, Charles F. Pfeiffer and Everett F. Harrison; Moody Press, 1962.

All biblical references are to the King James Version of the Holy Bible.

Made in the USA
Charleston, SC
21 June 2014